PIXEL PIONEERS: EXPLORING THE WORLD OF EMULATION GAMING

Pixel Pioneers: Exploring the World of Emulation Gaming

Exploring the World of Emulation Gaming

JONATHON ADRIANS

Better than Bonkers

CONTENTS

First Printing, 2024

ISBN: 979-8-8690-7961-9
EISBN: 979-8-8690-7962-6

| 1 |

Introduction to Emulation Gaming

In the expansive realm of gaming, one encounters a distinct and engrossing subculture known as emulation gaming. This subchapter will delve even deeper into the intricacies of this phenomenon, shedding light on its multifaceted nature and exploring its significance within the gaming community.

Emulation gaming, at its core, involves the art of replicating the hardware and software of older gaming systems on contemporary devices. This practice afford gamers the opportunity to bask in the charm and nostalgia of classic games that were originally designed for consoles and computers now deemed antiquated. Emulation enables gamers to relive the enchantment of retro console gaming, experience handheld gaming consoles, revel in vintage computers, and even indulge in specific consoles such as the NES or Sega Genesis.

One of the key drivers behind the surge in popularity of emulation gaming is its unmatched accessibility. Harnessing potent software, gamers can effortlessly transform their personal computers, smartphones, or dedicated devices into virtual versions of these bygone gaming machines. This liberation from the need to hunt for rare and costly vintage consoles or cartridges opens up a vast realm of possibilities. Emulation gaming extends an invitation to enthusiasts, beckoning them to explore titles they may have missed or revisit beloved classics with newfound vigor.

Beyond mere entertainment, emulation gaming has transcended into educational realms, assuming the role of a valuable teaching tool. Within academic settings, emulation serves as a conduit for understanding the history and evolution of gaming. The emulation of older systems offers students a profound insight into the technological advancements that have shaped the gaming industry over the years.

Furthermore, emulation gaming stands as a platform for dedicated enthusiasts to engage in the preservation and archiving of gaming history. The emulation community comprises passionate individuals who collaborate tirelessly to ensure that the games of yesteryear are not consigned to oblivion. Their unwavering dedication serves to preserve the cultural significance of these games, thereby making them accessible to future generations.

In conclusion, emulation gaming is not merely a pastime; it is a vibrant and immersive experience that beckons gamers, enthusiasts, and hobbyists alike to explore a wide array of gaming possibilities. Whether one seeks to relive the glory days of retro console gaming, uncover hidden gems from vintage computers, or employ emulation for educational purposes, this subculture acts as a bridge connecting the past with the present. It is a celebration of gaming history, fostering innovation and accessibility for all who embark on this nostalgic journey.

History and Evolution of Emulation Gaming: Unveiling the Tapestry of Time

Within the vast tapestry of gaming, nostalgia emerges as a potent thread, weaving through the hearts of gamers, enthusiasts, and hobbyists alike. It propels us back to an era when pixels reigned supreme, and gaming, though simpler, offered a thrilling experience. Emulation gaming emerges as a remarkable time machine, enabling us to revisit those cherished memories on modern devices. This subchapter embarks on an exploration of the captivating history and evolution of emulation gaming, unraveling its various niches and reflecting on the profound impact it has had on the gaming community.

The genesis of emulation gaming lies in retro console emulation. As technology evolved and gaming consoles transformed, the yearning to revisit classic games intensified. The advent of emulators heralded a new era in gaming, liberating players from the temporal and hardware constraints that once limited their gaming experience. Now, iconic titles from systems like the NES and Sega Genesis could be enjoyed on computers or even modern consoles, breaking down barriers and reshaping the gaming landscape.

Following in its footsteps, handheld gaming console emulation emerged, granting gamers the ability to relish classics from the Game Boy, Game Boy Advance, and other handheld devices on smartphones or tablets. This portable nostalgia allowed gaming enthusiasts to carry their favorite childhood games in their pockets, rekindling the joy and excitement of simpler times, even on the go.

Vintage computer emulation gaming elevated the emulation experience to new heights. From the early days of DOS games to the iconic Commodore 64, emulators unlocked the magic of vintage computer gaming. Running these historic games on modern hardware not only entertained but also educated players about the evolution of gaming technology, providing a treasure trove of forgotten gems.

The journey of emulation gaming extended into educational realms, where console-specific emulators found purpose. Educators recognized the potential of leveraging classic games as tools for learning, engaging students with history, science, and various subjects in a unique and interactive manner.

Undoubtedly, the history and evolution of emulation gaming have left an indelible mark on the gaming landscape. It has rekindled the flame of retro gaming, allowed exploration of consoles and computers missed in the past, and presented an innovative approach to education. As the emulation community continues to push boundaries, refining the accuracy and performance of emulators, the gaming world remains forever indebted to this extraordinary technology.

Whether one is a seasoned gamer or a curious enthusiast, the world of emulation gaming extends an invitation to traverse the corridors of the past.

It beckons you to relive the golden age of gaming, rediscover forgotten classics, and embrace the nostalgia that accompanies pixelated history.

Benefits and Drawbacks of Emulation Gaming: Navigating the Pixelated Landscape

The rising popularity of emulation gaming has cast its allure upon gamers, enthusiasts, and hobbyists alike. This subchapter endeavors to unravel the intricate tapestry of benefits and drawbacks woven into the fabric of this unique gaming experience, catering to a diverse audience encompassing retro console emulation gaming, handheld gaming console emulation, vintage computer emulation gaming, console-specific emulation (e.g., NES, Sega Genesis), and emulation gaming for educational purposes.

At the forefront of the myriad benefits lies the unparalleled ability to revisit classic games from the annals of gaming history. Retro console emulation gaming acts as a portal, allowing players to immerse themselves in the nostalgia of iconic games like Super Mario Bros, The Legend of Zelda, or Sonic the Hedgehog. This opens up a new frontier of gaming for those who may have missed out on these timeless classics during their original release.

Handheld gaming console emulation elevates the gaming experience further, offering players the chance to enjoy their favorite portable titles on a single device. Whether relishing Pokémon on the Game Boy or delving into Final Fantasy on the PSP, emulation provides the convenience of carrying multiple games in one's pocket without the need for multiple consoles.

Vintage computer emulation gaming serves as a conduit to the history of technology and gaming. Enthusiasts can explore the early days of computing, experiencing games that were groundbreaking in their time. This form of emulation gaming not only entertains but also imparts knowledge about the evolution of gaming technology, providing a holistic understanding.

Console-specific emulation, such as NES or

Sega Genesis emulation, presents an avenue for gamers to indulge in titles from specific consoles without the need for original hardware. This not only saves money and space but also ensures an authentic gaming experience, preserving the essence of the past.

Emulation gaming for educational purposes stands out as a prominent benefit. Teachers and students alike can leverage emulation software to delve into the history of gaming, comprehend game design principles, and even hone their programming skills. By simulating the hardware and software of older systems, emulation becomes a valuable tool within the classroom, transcending the boundaries of traditional education.

However, in the quest for pixelated perfection, one must acknowledge the drawbacks inherent in emulation gaming. Legal concerns loom over certain forms of emulation, entangled in the complexities of copying and distributing copyrighted material. Additionally, the accuracy of emulation can be a variable, leading to occasional bugs or glitches that may impact the overall gaming experience.

In conclusion, emulation gaming stands as a compelling choice, offering an array of benefits ranging from nostalgia and convenience to educational opportunities. While potential drawbacks exist, the overarching appeal and accessibility of emulation gaming make it an enticing option for those eager to explore the realm of classic games and gaming history.

| **2** |

Retro Console Emulation Gaming

Overview of Retro Console Emulation: A Deeper Dive into Nostalgia

Within the dynamic landscape of gaming, a burgeoning trend is capturing the hearts of players, gaming enthusiasts, and hobbyists — the ability to revive the nostalgia of cherished retro consoles and games through emulation. Retro console emulation has blossomed into a phenomenon, drawing immense popularity and fostering a bridge between the past and the present. With technological advancements, enthusiasts can now recreate the gaming ambiance of classic consoles and vintage computers on contemporary devices.

At its essence, emulation gaming involves replicating the hardware and software of retro gaming consoles on a diverse range of platforms, such as computers or handheld devices. This is made possible through specialized software known as emulators, allowing gamers to traverse through the realms of the Nintendo Entertainment System (NES), Sega Genesis, or even vintage computers like the Commodore 64.

A particularly enthralling facet of retro console emulation is the capability to resurrect handheld gaming experiences. Emulators catering to handheld devices such as the Game Boy, Game Boy Advance, and the venerable Nintendo DS are readily available. This empowers users to indulge in their favorite handheld games on smartphones or tablets, unlocking a treasure trove of gaming possibilities that can be carried conveniently in one's pocket.

Delving into the realm of vintage computer

emulation gaming unveils another layer of the emulation experience. Emulators designed for computers like the Amiga, Atari ST, and ZX Spectrum rekindle the golden age of computing and gaming, allowing enthusiasts to immerse themselves in the software and games that once represented cutting-edge technology.

Retro console emulation has not confined itself to the realm of entertainment alone; it has found its way into educational settings. Educators and students alike leverage emulators to delve into gaming history, study game design principles, and even venture into programming by examining the code of classic games. Emulation gaming for educational purposes offers a unique and interactive approach to learning about the evolution of technology and its profound impact on society.

In conclusion, retro console emulation has evolved into a beloved pastime, offering a diverse range of experiences for gamers, enthusiasts, and hobbyists. Whether one seeks to relive cherished childhood memories, explore the rich tapestry of gaming history, or employ emulators for educational pursuits, the world of retro console emulation invites individuals to embark on a journey through the pixelated wonders of the past.

Popular Retro Consoles for Emulation: A Symphony of Nostalgia

Emulation gaming has become a cherished pastime, captivating gamers, enthusiasts, and hobbyists in its nostalgic embrace. The ability to resurrect classic games on modern devices has opened a gateway to a realm of nostalgic fun. This subchapter embarks on a journey through some of the most beloved retro consoles for emulation, catering to a diverse spectrum of gaming interests and niches.

Handheld gaming consoles hold a special place in the hearts of many gamers. From the iconic Game Boy to the lesser-known Atari Lynx, these portable devices provided hours of entertainment on the go. Today, with the marvels of emulation technology, gamers can relive these handheld classics on smartphones, tablets, or dedicated handheld emulation devices.

Venturing into the niche of vintage computer emulation gaming unveils a trove of iconic systems that left an indelible mark on the gaming industry. The Commodore 64, Amiga, and ZX Spectrum stand as testaments to an era where computing and gaming intertwined. Emulating these systems grants gamers an opportunity to delve into the rich history of computer gaming, experiencing titles that laid the foundation for contemporary games.

Console-specific emulation, a thriving niche within the emulation gaming community, pays homage to iconic systems such as the Nintendo Entertainment System (NES) and the Sega Genesis. Each console boasts a unique library of games that have endured the test of time. Emulation allows gamers to revel in these classic titles without the need for original hardware, rendering the experience accessible to a wider audience.

Emulation gaming extends beyond mere entertainment; it has found its place in education. Vintage computer emulators, for instance, provide a means to explore the history of computing and comprehend the evolution of technology. These emulators serve as portals to early operating systems, programming languages, and software applications, offering a glimpse into the past and fostering a deeper understanding of the digital world.

In conclusion, the realm of retro console emulation unfolds a myriad of options for gamers, enthusiasts, and hobbyists. Whether one harbors a fondness for handheld gaming, vintage computers, console-specific nostalgia, or seeks to harness emulation for educational purposes, there exists an emulation solution catering to diverse interests. By tapping into the wonders of emulation, individuals can relive the enchantment of classic games and explore the rich history of gaming in an accessible and convenient manner. Happy gaming!

Setting Up and Configuring Retro Console Emulators: Crafting Your Pixelated Wonderland

In the exhilarating realm of emulation gaming,

few experiences match the joy of reliving classic retro console games. Technological advancements have empowered gamers, enthusiasts, and hobbyists to effortlessly recreate the magic of vintage gaming on their contemporary devices. This subchapter serves as a guiding light, walking you through the process of setting up and configuring retro console emulators, allowing you to immerse yourself in the golden era of gaming.

Embarking on your emulation gaming journey necessitates selecting the right emulator for your chosen console. Whether you harbor a penchant for the NES, Sega Genesis, or any other console, a plethora of reliable emulators awaits online. Opt for popular and well-maintained emulators that offer a broad range of features and compatibility with your preferred gaming system.

With your chosen emulator in hand, the next step involves configuring it to provide an optimal gaming experience. Commence by adjusting the graphics settings to align with your device's capabilities and personal preferences. Some emulators offer a plethora of filters and shader options designed to enhance the visual quality of games. Experimenting with these settings allows you to strike the perfect balance between nostalgia and modern visual enhancements.

Following graphics configuration, the next pivotal step is configuring the controller settings. Most emulators provide the flexibility to map the buttons of your modern controller to mirror the layout of the original console. This ensures seamless gameplay and an authentic retro feel. For those yearning for the classic experience, consider using USB adapters to connect original controllers to your device.

For an even deeper dive into the emulation gaming experience, explore the realm of console-specific emulation. Each console boasts unique features and quirks that can be faithfully replicated through specialized emulators. Whether it's the distinctive sound chip of the iconic NES or the blast processing power of the Sega Genesis, console-specific emulators promise an unparalleled gaming experience.

Beyond recreation, emulation gaming unfolds as a valuable educational tool. Numerous vintage computer emulators facilitate exploration of the history of computing and understanding the evolution of technology. These emulators provide a chance to experience early operating systems, programming languages, and software applications, offering a glimpse into the past and fostering a profound understanding of the digital world.

In conclusion, the process of setting up and configuring retro console emulators opens a gateway to a realm of possibilities for gamers, enthusiasts, and hobbyists. Whether your pursuit is grounded in pure entertainment or educational endeavors, this subchapter lays a foundation to embark on your emulation gaming adventure. So, seize your controller, load up your favorite games, and get ready to relive the magic of retro gaming in the modern era.

Exploring Retro Console Emulation

Gaming Communities: Unveiling the Tapestry of Enthusiasm

Retro console emulation gaming has evolved into a dynamic and thriving community within the expansive realm of gaming.

As technology advances, the innate desire to revisit and experience classic games on their original consoles has spurred the rise of emulation gaming. This subchapter seeks to delve deeper into the myriad facets of this captivating world, shedding light on the communities that have organically formed around it.

One of the most enchanting aspects of retro console emulation gaming lies in the ability to traverse games from different eras and platforms. Whether one is a fervent fan of the NES, Sega Genesis, or vintage computer games, emulation allows enthusiasts to relive these experiences on modern devices. The communities revolving around specific console emulations are passionate and dedicated, consistently sharing insights, strategies, and even custom modifications to elevate the gaming experience.

Handheld gaming console emulation has witnessed substantial popularity in recent years. With the advent of potent smartphones and handheld devices, gamers can now savor their cherished Game Boy or PSP titles on the go. These communities buzz with enthusiasts who engage in discussions about optimal emulators, recommended games, and even provide tutorials on optimizing emulation settings for peak performance.

Beyond the realms of recreation, emulation gaming has found a meaningful place in education. Educators have harnessed the potential of retro console emulation to impart lessons about gaming history, game design, and even computer programming. The educational communities nestled within the emulation gaming sphere tirelessly share resources and lesson plans, making it more accessible for educators to integrate this innovative approach into their classrooms.

In addition to console-specific emulation communities, overarching emulation gaming communities bring together gamers from diverse niches.

These communities serve as bustling hubs for discussions, game recommendations, and troubleshooting. Often hosting events like online tournaments or challenges, these communities foster a sense of camaraderie among members who share a common passion for retro console emulation gaming.

In conclusion, the exploration of retro console emulation gaming communities unfurls a realm of endless possibilities for gamers, enthusiasts, and hobbyists. Whether you seek to relive the nostalgia of your youth or unearth the classics that shaped gaming history, these communities provide a space for like-minded individuals to connect, share, and celebrate the art of emulation gaming. Dive into the world of retro console emulation gaming communities, and unlock a treasure trove of gaming experiences!

| 3 |

Handheld Gaming Console Emulation

Introduction to Handheld Gaming Console Emulation: Unveiling Nostalgic Realms

In the enchanting world of gaming, nostalgia stands as a potent force, propelling our passion for beloved games. Handheld gaming consoles, such as the iconic Game Boy or Sega Game Gear, hold a unique place in our hearts, evoking memories of hours immersed in virtual worlds. Yet, as technology strides forward, these devices become relics, leaving cherished moments stranded in the past. This is where handheld gaming console emulation emerges as a savior.

Handheld gaming console emulation is a gateway to recreate the experience of playing favorite handheld games on modern devices like smartphones, tablets, or computers. A captivating and innovative technology, it has garnered popularity among gamers, enthusiasts, and hobbyists, offering a bridge between the past and the present.

A pivotal advantage of handheld gaming console emulation lies in the ability to access a diverse array of games from different consoles in one place. Instead of investing in multiple physical devices, emulation allows for the consolidation of these consoles into software, providing a vast library of games at one's fingertips. Whether one seeks to revisit classics or unearth hidden gems, emulation unfolds an extensive catalog of games to explore.

Moreover, handheld gaming console emulation serves as a guardian of gaming history. Vintage consoles and their games face the risk of physical deterioration over time. Emulation steps in to create digital copies, ensuring the longevity and accessibility of these games for future generations. It becomes a portal to experience games from consoles that might have been out of reach in the past.

Beyond entertainment, emulation gaming, including handheld console emulation, extends its reach into educational realms. Educators can leverage emulation to impart lessons about gaming history, game design, and programming. By delving into and analyzing games of the past, students gain a profound understanding of the evolution of technology and its societal impact.

This book, "Pixel Pioneers: Exploring the World of Emulation Gaming," will immerse readers in the captivating realm of handheld gaming console emulation. It delves into various emulators, offers best practices for setting up and using emulation software, and navigates the legal and ethical considerations surrounding emulation. Specific console emulators, such as NES, Sega Genesis, and Game Boy, will be examined to provide a comprehensive understanding of the myriad possibilities that emulation gaming unfolds.

Whether one is a gamer, gaming enthusiast, or gaming hobbyist, this book aims to reignite the passion for emulation gaming and inspire a journey through the rich history of handheld gaming consoles. Let's embark on an exploration of handheld gaming console emulation and relive the magic of our favorite games from the past.

Noteworthy Handheld Gaming Consoles for Emulation: Portals to Nostalgic Realities

In the expansive landscape of emulation gaming, handheld consoles occupy a cherished realm. These portable devices not only offer a means to relive the nostalgia of classic games on the go but also unlock a gateway to the world of retro console emulation gaming. Whether one is a gaming enthusiast, a hobbyist, or someone intrigued by educational facets, several noteworthy handheld gaming consoles shine as perfect candidates for emulation.

At the forefront of handheld console emulation

is the Nintendo Game Boy Advance (GBA). Released in 2001, the GBA boasts a rich library of games and supports emulation for various retro consoles. Its compact size and diverse game selection make the GBA a favorite among gamers and emulation enthusiasts alike.

Another standout handheld console for emulation is the Sony PlayStation Portable (PSP), launched in 2004. Beyond being a powerful gaming device, the PSP features the ability to emulate various retro consoles, including the NES and Sega Genesis. Its expansive screen and multimedia capabilities make it an excellent choice for gaming on the move.

For aficionados of vintage computer emulation gaming, the ZX Spectrum Vega takes the stage. Tailored for games from the ZX Spectrum era, this handheld console provides a nostalgic experience for retro gaming enthusiasts. With a built-in library of over 1,000 games and the capability to load additional titles through an SD card, the ZX Spectrum Vega is a must-have for emulation gaming hobbyists.

Additionally, for those intrigued by console-specific emulation, compact handheld devices like the BittBoy PocketGo or RetroArch step up to the plate. Supporting a broad range of retro consoles such as the NES and Sega Genesis, these devices promise an authentic gaming experience with retro-inspired designs and user-friendly interfaces.

Beyond recreational gaming, emulation gaming holds educational value. Handheld consoles like the Arduboy and PocketSprite can be utilized for educational purposes, teaching programming and game development skills. These devices empower users to create and play their own games, fostering creativity and learning in a compact and portable format.

From the timeless Game Boy Advance to the versatile Sony PSP, and from console-specific handhelds to educational devices, the realm of handheld gaming consoles for emulation is expansive and thrilling. These devices not only rekindle the joy of playing retro games but also offer a platform for delving into the history of gaming and nurturing creative skills. Whether one is a gaming enthusiast, hobbyist, or an advocate of educational gaming, these noteworthy handheld consoles promise hours of entertainment and exploration.

Emulating Handheld Gaming Consoles on Different Platforms: Unleashing Nostalgia Everywhere

In the vast expanse of emulation gaming, a thrilling realm beckons gamers to rediscover the joy of their favorite handheld gaming consoles. From the iconic Game Boy to the groundbreaking PlayStation Portable, these handheld devices, etched in the hearts of gamers, can now be experienced on various platforms through the magic of emulation.

Emulation gaming unfolds as the process of replicating the hardware and software of a gaming console on diverse platforms, such as a PC, smartphone, or even a Raspberry Pi. This enables gamers to play the original games from beloved handheld consoles without the need for the physical device itself. It's a captivating means to preserve gaming history and relive the magic of these handhelds in contemporary settings.

Among the plethora of platforms, the PC emerges as a popular choice for handheld console emulation. With the right emulator software, gamers can relish games from consoles like the Game Boy, Game Boy Advance, and Nintendo DS on their desktop or laptop computers. This introduces a realm of possibilities, as PC gaming offers superior graphics, customizable controls, and the ability to save and load games at any moment. It's the perfect medium to experience classic handheld games with a new and enhanced perspective.

Smartphones, too, have transformed into potent gaming devices, and they are not exempt from the embrace of handheld console emulation. Emulator apps, available for both iOS and Android devices, allow gamers to carry their beloved handheld games wherever they go. Whether it's Pokemon or Super Mario, the entire library of handheld classics is now at their fingertips.

For those captivated by vintage computer gaming, emulators are available for platforms such as the Commodore 64, Atari Lynx, and Neo Geo Pocket. These emulators resurrect the experience of playing games on these vintage computers, offering gamers a chance to rediscover the charm and simplicity of early gaming.

Emulation gaming extends beyond entertainment; it bears educational value. Teachers and educators can utilize console-specific emulators, such as those for the NES or Sega Genesis, to impart lessons about gaming history and the evolution of technology. By exploring the games and hardware of the past, students can gain a deeper understanding of the gaming industry and its cultural impact.

In conclusion, emulating handheld gaming consoles on different platforms is a thrilling endeavor for gamers, enthusiasts, and hobbyists alike. Whether it's on a PC, smartphone, or vintage computer, the ability to play these cherished games unfurls a world of possibilities. Emulation gaming invites us to revisit the past, explore gaming history, and forge new memories in the digital realm. So, grab the favorite handheld console, fire up an emulator, and let the gaming nostalgia unfold!

Tips and Tricks for Optimal Handheld Gaming Emulation Experience: Elevating Nostalgic Journeys

In the realm of gaming, a burgeoning trend fueled by nostalgia enthusiasts has emerged, delighting in the rediscovery of retro gaming's golden days. Thanks to the marvels of emulation technology, the joy of playing classic handheld games on modern devices is now within reach. Whether one is a seasoned gamer or a novice venturing into the world of emulation gaming, here are some tips and tricks to enhance the handheld gaming emulation experience.

1. Choose the Right Emulator: The emulation landscape is teeming with options, each with its strengths and weaknesses. Research and explore various emulators to find the one that aligns with your preferences. Consider factors like compatibility, performance, and customization options.

2. Controller Configuration: For an authentic retro gaming experience, consider using a controller that mimics the original handheld device. Many modern controllers are compatible with emulators and can be configured to replicate the button layout of the original consoles.

3. Graphics and Sound Enhancement: Emulators often come with options to enhance graphics and sound. Experiment with different settings to strike the right balance between nostalgia and visual/audio quality. Some emulators even offer filters to recreate the original handheld screen's look and feel.

4. ROM Selection: Emulation relies on ROMs, digital copies of original game cartridges. Ensure you obtain ROMs legally and from trusted sources. Organize your ROM collection for easier navigation and access.

5. Save States and Fast Forwarding: Emulators commonly offer a save state feature, allowing you to save your progress at any point and resume later. Additionally, a fast-forward option can be handy for skipping repetitive sections or speeding up gameplay.

6. Customization and Cheats: Explore emulator features for customization, such as screen filters, aspect ratio adjustments, and control mapping. Tailor your gaming experience to your liking. Some emulators support cheat codes, providing opportunities to unlock hidden features or gain advantages in the game.

7. Emulation for Educational Purposes: Emulation gaming extends beyond entertainment and serves as an excellent tool for education. Vintage computer emulators, for instance, offer a plethora of educational software and games that can teach programming, history, and various subjects.

By incorporating these tips and tricks, you can optimize your handheld gaming emulation experience and embark on an immersive journey through the world of retro gaming. Whether you're revisiting cherished memories or exploring classics for the first time, emulation gaming offers boundless possibilities for gamers, enthusiasts, and hobbyists alike.

| 4 |

Vintage Computer Emulation Gaming

Understanding Vintage Computer Emulation: A Dive into Gaming History

In the ever-evolving landscape of gaming, the allure of vintage computer emulation has enraptured gamers, enthusiasts, and hobbyists alike. Technological advancements now allow us to recreate the enchantment of old-school gaming on contemporary devices. This subchapter aims to illuminate the captivating world of vintage computer emulation and its diverse applications.

Vintage computer emulation gaming unfolds

as a portal to a nostalgic journey, inviting players to experience the iconic games of bygone eras. By simulating the hardware and software of vintage computers like the Commodore 64, Amiga, and Atari systems, emulation enables gamers to relive the golden age of gaming. The magic lies in the faithful reproduction of gameplay, graphics, and sound, preserving the timeless essence of these classic games.

Within the realm of vintage computer emulation, retro console emulation gaming stands as a distinct niche. This focus revolves around recreating the experience of playing games on retro consoles, from the legendary NES to the beloved Sega Genesis. With a simple click, gamers can resurrect cherished childhood memories, engaging in classics like Super Mario Bros., Sonic the Hedgehog, and Street Fighter II on modern devices.

Taking the nostalgia factor to new heights, handheld gaming console emulation replicates the experience of portable gaming devices such as the Game Boy and PSP. Now, gamers can carry an extensive library of retro games in their pockets, immersing themselves in the familiar gameplay of titles like Pokémon Red, Super Mario Land, and Metal Gear Solid: Peace Walker.

However, vintage computer emulation gaming isn't solely about revisiting the past; it has found its place in educational settings as well. Both teachers and students can leverage emulation gaming for educational purposes, delving into the evolution of technology and gaming. Through the study of programming and hardware in vintage computers, students gain a profound understanding of the technological advancements that have shaped the gaming industry.

Console-specific emulation takes a focused approach, emulating a particular gaming console to provide an authentic experience for dedicated fans. Whether it's the immersive world of NES or the groundbreaking graphics of the Sega Genesis, console-specific emulation caters to the needs of enthusiasts who seek to relive the unique characteristics of their favorite consoles.

In conclusion, vintage computer emulation has

revolutionized the gaming world, offering enthusiasts a chance to delve into the rich history of gaming and relish the magic of retro games. From the rekindling of childhood memories to the exploration of the educational value of vintage computers, this subchapter has provided a glimpse into the thrilling world of vintage computer emulation gaming.

Emulating Popular Vintage Computers: Reliving the Golden Age

Vintage computers hold a special place in the hearts of many gamers and enthusiasts. These machines, with their nostalgic charm and unique software libraries, offer a peek into the early days of computing and gaming. Thanks to emulation, it's now possible to experience these classic systems right on your modern computer or handheld device.

Emulation gaming has become immensely popular, providing an avenue for gamers to relive cherished childhood memories or discover gaming gems of yesteryears. One exciting facet of emulation is the ability to emulate popular vintage computers like the Commodore 64, Amiga, or Atari ST. These systems had distinct personalities and software catalogs that are worth exploring.

By emulating vintage computers, gamers gain access to a diverse range of classic games and software that defined a generation. Whether you want to relive the pixelated adventures of Pac-Man or immerse yourself in text-based interactive fiction, vintage computer emulation has something for everyone. These systems featured unique hardware capabilities often overlooked, such as advanced sound chips or sprite capabilities, adding a new layer of appreciation to the gaming experience.

Vintage computer emulation for educational purposes is another exciting niche. Many schools and universities are utilizing emulation software to teach computer science or digital art courses. By emulating popular vintage computers, students can learn about programming, graphic design, and game development using the tools and languages of the past. It's a fantastic bridge between the present and the past, allowing students to gain a deeper understanding of technology's evolution.

In conclusion, vintage computer emulation gaming offers a chance for gamers, enthusiasts, and hobbyists to relive the golden age of computing and gaming. With the ability to emulate popular systems like the Commodore 64 or the Amiga, gamers can explore a vast library of classic games and software. Moreover, vintage computer emulation has proven to be a valuable educational tool, enabling students to learn about the foundations of computer science and digital art. So, dust off those virtual floppy disks and get ready to journey back in time with vintage computer emulation gaming.

Configuring Vintage Computer Emulators: A Guide to Nostalgic Adventures

Vintage computer emulation gaming allows players to bask in the nostalgia of older computer systems and games. With technological advancements, gamers can now recreate the magic of retro gaming on their modern devices. This subchapter serves as a guide, walking you through the process of configuring vintage computer emulators to relive the golden age of computing.

To embark on this journey, let's first explore the different types of vintage computer emulation available. Emulation gaming spans a wide spectrum, encompassing retro console emulation gaming, handheld gaming console emulation, and vintage computer emulation gaming. Whether you're eager to play classic NES games or yearning for the thrill of old-school Commodore 64 titles, there's an emulator catering to every gaming enthusiast.

A notable category within emulation is console-specific emulation, focusing on replicating the experience of specific consoles like NES, Sega Genesis, or Atari 2600. These emulators aim to faithfully reproduce the hardware and software of the original consoles, allowing you to immerse yourself in games exactly as they were intended.

Beyond entertainment, emulation gaming serves educational purposes. Vintage computer emulation offers a unique opportunity to learn about the origins of computing and explore the evolution of technology. By configuring emulators and experimenting with different software, you can gain a deeper understanding of the history of computers and gaming.

Now, let's delve into the process of configuring vintage computer emulators. The first step is choosing the right emulator for your desired platform. Popular choices include DOSBox, MAME, or Vice (for Commodore 64). Once downloaded, you'll need to obtain the appropriate ROMs or disk images of the games you want to play. Numerous websites dedicated to preserving retro gaming offer these files.

With the necessary files in hand, you can begin configuring the emulator settings. This may involve adjusting graphics, audio, and input settings to optimize your gaming experience. Many emulators come with additional features such as save states, cheat code support, and controller customization, enabling you to tailor your gameplay to your preferences.

In conclusion, configuring vintage computer emulators unlocks a realm of possibilities for gamers, enthusiasts, and hobbyists. Whether you're revisiting cherished memories or exploring the roots of gaming for educational purposes, emulation gaming offers an exciting journey through the history of computing. Follow the steps outlined in this subchapter to embark on your own adventure into the world of vintage computer emulation gaming.

Exploring Classic Computer Games and Software Libraries: A Journey Through Gaming History

Classic computer games stand as timeless artifacts, weaving tales of nostalgia that resonate with gamers, enthusiasts, and hobbyists. These gems from the past have not only shaped the gaming industry but continue to captivate players across generations. In this subchapter, we immerse ourselves in the world of classic computer games and the software libraries that breathe life into them through the marvel of emulation gaming.

Emulation gaming emerges as a revolutionary force, transforming the way we engage with retro games. By emulating vintage consoles and computers, gamers can resurrect the enchantment of iconic titles, unburdened by the constraints of original hardware. From the emulation of retro consoles to the recreation of handheld gaming experiences, the possibilities are boundless.

One of the most thrilling facets of emulation gaming lies in the expansive array of software libraries available. These repositories house an impressive collection of games, spanning from enduring classics to hidden gems waiting to be rediscovered. Whether your heart beats for console-specific emulation like NES or Sega Genesis, or you're drawn into the realm of vintage computer emulation gaming, there exists a treasure trove catering to every gaming palate.

Emulation gaming isn't merely a source of entertainment; it is also a vessel of educational value. Enthusiasts and educators alike leverage emulation gaming to study the evolution of technology and game design. By peeling back the layers of gaming history and deciphering the mechanics behind these classics, a profound appreciation for the industry's progression emerges.

Throughout this subchapter, we embark on a journey through various software libraries dedicated to emulation gaming. Our exploration delves into the diverse platforms and consoles they support, spotlighting standout titles and uncovering hidden gems within each library. From the charming simplicity of the 8-bit era to the groundbreaking strides of the 16-bit generation, our odyssey spans the entirety of gaming's rich tapestry.

Whether you're a seasoned veteran in the realm of gaming or a newcomer eager to delve into the wonders of emulation gaming, this subchapter unfolds as a treasure trove of insights and recommendations. We delve into the significance of preserving gaming history, navigate the legal landscape of emulation gaming, and guide you on initiating your emulation setup.

Join us on this immersive journey through

time as we explore the profound legacy of classic computer games and the software libraries that serve as their eternal guardians. Prepare to relive the magic and embark on new adventures as we plunge into the captivating world of emulation gaming. The past awaits your rediscovery.

| 5 |

Console-Specific Emulation

NES Emulation Gaming: A Journey Into Nostalgic Wonderland

The NES (Nintendo Entertainment System) stands as an everlasting legend in the vast tapestry of gaming history, heralded for its pivotal role in revolutionizing the industry and igniting a golden age of video games. The iconic gray box, adorned with simplicity yet boasting addictive gameplay, etched itself into the hearts of gamers globally. While the original hardware may now be elusive, the marvels of emulation gaming unfurl an opportunity to rekindle the enchantment of the NES.

Emulation gaming, a practice akin to techno-logical time travel, involves employing software to resurrect the hardware and software intricacies of a specific gaming console or computer system. NES emulation gaming, in particular, becomes a vessel for transporting the joy of the NES to a new generation of players.

For aficionados of retro consoles, NES emulation gaming offers a portal to relive cherished childhood memories and rediscover the games that laid the foundation for the industry. Whether navigating the treacherous landscapes of Super Mario Bros., embarking on a quest to save Hyrule in The Legend of Zelda, or engaging in fisticuffs in the original Punch-Out!!, NES emulation gaming facilitates an effortless voyage into these timeless classics.

Taking the allure of nostalgia a step further, handheld gaming console emulation invites play-ers to experience NES games on portable devices. Picture immersing yourself in the world of Super Mario Bros. during your daily commute or indulg-ing in a session of Duck Hunt on a handheld gaming console during an extended road trip. The possibilities are boundless, and the convenience of relishing NES games on-the-go is truly extraordinary.

Beyond being a conduit for entertainment, NES emulation gaming unfurls its educational wings. By delving into the intricacies of game mechanics, level design, and storytelling techniques embedded in NES games, aspiring game developers can glean invaluable insights into the foundational aspects of the gaming industry. NES emulation gaming, therefore, emerges not just as an entertainment medium but as a powerful learning tool for those venturing into the realms of game design, programming, or seeking a deeper comprehension of the evolution of video games.

Whether you're an unwavering gamer, a casual gaming hobbyist, or simply harbor curiosity about the vast realm of emulation gaming, the expedition into NES emulation gaming promises an adventure worth savoring. From the enchanting 8-bit graphics to the indelible soundtracks, this subchapter serves as a compass guiding you through the wonders of NES emulation gaming, offering not just tips and recommendations but also insights into the best games, emulators, and platforms. Brace yourself for a nostalgic odyssey, and prepare to relive the glory days of gaming with NES emulation gaming!

Sega Genesis Emulation Gaming: Unveiling the Charms of Retro Reverie

In the vast cosmos of retro gaming, a distinct charm and nostalgia envelop the exploration of classic consoles and games of yesteryear. Among these, the Sega Genesis stands out as a luminary, captivating the hearts of gamers with its iconic games and innovative technology that reverberates even in contemporary times.

Sega Genesis emulation gaming, a technological ballet, facilitates the reliving of the magic contained within this beloved console on modern devices. The process of emulation gaming, a digital resurrection of hardware and software, emancipates gamers from the constraints of the original console, opening avenues for the seamless enjoyment of cherished Sega Genesis titles.

For enthusiasts dedicated to retro consoles, Sega Genesis emulation gaming offers not only a convenient but also a cost-effective avenue to savor classic titles. Instead of embarking on quests to hunt down elusive cartridges or grappling with aging hardware, gamers can simply download emulator software and ROMs (game files) to embark on a journey through the Sega Genesis library from the comfort of their own devices.

The allure extends further with handheld gaming console emulation, injecting mobility into the Sega Genesis gaming experience. With the proliferation of smartphones and portable gaming devices, Sega Genesis enthusiasts can carry their favorite titles wherever they go. Whether battling Dr. Robotnik in Sonic the Hedgehog or delving into the mystical realms of Altered Beast, handheld emulation beckons gamers to experience the Sega Genesis magic on the move.

Sega Genesis emulation gaming transcends

mere entertainment; it becomes a conduit for educational exploration. Laden with rich history and cultural significance, studying the development and impact of the Sega Genesis unveils valuable insights into the broader evolution of gaming. The emulation platform becomes a scholarly tool, enabling students and researchers to delve into the technical nuances of the console, explore its game library, and contextualize the cultural tapestry surrounding Sega's ascent to prominence.

In conclusion, Sega Genesis emulation gaming emerges as a favored choice among gamers, gaming enthusiasts, and hobbyists alike. Whether you identify as a retro console aficionado, a handheld gaming enthusiast, or a researcher delving into the annals of gaming history, the realm of Sega Genesis emulation gaming unfolds as a vast playground catering to myriad interests. So, grasp your controller, ignite your emulator, and immerse yourself in a nostalgic journey through the golden age of gaming.

Super Nintendo Emulation Gaming: Unveiling Timeless Wonders

Emulation gaming, weaving a tapestry of joy and nostalgia, has become a cherished pastime for gamers, enthusiasts, and hobbyists alike. Among the pantheon of consoles celebrated in this digital renaissance, the Super Nintendo Entertainment System (SNES) emerges as an icon. This subchapter beckons you into the realm of Super Nintendo emulation gaming, offering a kaleidoscope of opportunities for rediscovering the magic of a bygone era.

The popularity of retro console emulation gaming has surged in recent years, riding the crest of technological advancements. Today, it is not merely a dream but a tangible reality to recreate the nostalgic essence of classic SNES games on modern devices. Whether you yearn to rekindle the flames of childhood memories or embark on a maiden voyage into the enchanting world of retro gaming, Super Nintendo emulation gaming unfurls itself as a gateway to a bygone epoch.

Handheld gaming console emulation stands as

a particularly thrilling facet of SNES emulation gaming. Armed with the right amalgamation of software and hardware, your smartphone or tablet transforms into a portable SNES gaming haven. Picture yourself playing Super Mario World or The Legend of Zelda: A Link to the Past on-the-go, capturing the essence of handheld gaming from the '90s in the palm of your hand.

The exploration of vintage computer emulation gaming extends beyond the confines of consoles. The SNES, with its array of fantastic computer ports, beckons enthusiasts to relive classics like SimCity, Lemmings, or Prince of Persia on a modern PC. This multi-dimensional approach to SNES emulation gaming encapsulates not just the console experience but expands into the rich tapestry of computer gaming.

Console-specific emulation, a focal point in the emulation gaming landscape, reaches new heights with Super Nintendo emulation gaming. It invites enthusiasts to traverse the vast library of SNES games, immersing themselves in the unique gameplay experiences that defined an era of gaming.

This nuanced approach sets the stage for a profound exploration of the gaming landscape, offering a trip down memory lane and a window into the evolution of gaming experiences.

Beyond its role as an entertainment medium, SNES emulation gaming unfurls educational vistas. Teachers and students can harness the potential of SNES emulation for pedagogical purposes, exploring the historical significance of video games, dissecting game design principles, or even venturing into the realm of creating their own games. SNES emulation emerges not just as a portal to the past but as a powerful educational tool, engaging students and fostering creativity.

In conclusion, Super Nintendo emulation gaming unfurls a world of possibilities for gamers of all stripes. Whether you're a devoted retro enthusiast, a handheld gaming connoisseur, or a hobbyist eager to explore the annals of gaming, SNES emulation gaming promises to captivate your imagination. So, seize your controller, kindle your emulator, and prepare to embark on a journey through the pixelated landscapes of your favorite Super Nintendo classics.

PlayStation Emulation Gaming: Bridging Eras Through Virtual Realms

In the vast tapestry of gaming, few consoles have left as profound a mark as the PlayStation. From its groundbreaking debut in the mid-1990s to the cutting-edge models of today, the PlayStation has woven itself into the hearts and minds of gamers worldwide. What if you could revisit those cherished gaming moments without the constraints of the original hardware? Welcome to the immersive world of PlayStation emulation gaming.

Emulation gaming, where technology meets nostalgia, stands as a fascinating realm. It extends an invitation to gamers to partake in classic titles from various console generations on modern devices. PlayStation emulation opens a realm of endless possibilities, catering to retro console enthusiasts, handheld gaming aficionados, and even vintage computer gaming enthusiasts.

The allure of PlayStation emulation gaming lies in its ability to bring forth games from diverse generations of consoles. From the iconic PlayStation 1 to the beloved PlayStation 2 and the more recent PlayStation 3, emulation offers a passport to traverse these gaming epochs. Picture yourself reliving the magic of Final Fantasy VII, navigating the intricate plots of Metal Gear Solid, or embracing the adrenaline rush of Gran Turismo, all within the digital embrace of your PC or smartphone.

PlayStation emulation gaming transcends mere nostalgia; it evolves into a conduit for unique educational opportunities. Institutions from schools to universities have begun incorporating emulation gaming into their curricula. It serves as a tool to teach programming, game design, and history, offering an immersive and interactive approach for students to explore the evolution of gaming technology and its profound impact on society.

Console-specific emulation, whether it be NES, Sega Genesis, or PlayStation, brings forth a gateway to explore the rich histories of these iconic systems. PlayStation emulation, in particular, acts as an inclusive force, making these games accessible to a wider audience and ensuring the preservation of gaming heritage.

Whether you're a gaming hobbyist, an ardent enthusiast, or simply someone yearning to bask in the nostalgia of classic PlayStation titles, PlayStation emulation gaming has a bounty to offer. It acts as a portal to a vast library of games, a bridge connecting gaming eras, and an opportunity to learn, explore, and rediscover the profound impact of gaming on culture and society. So, grab your favorite controller, and prepare to embark on an unforgettable journey into the realms of PlayStation emulation gaming.

Xbox Emulation Gaming: Reliving the Odyssey of Gaming's Evolution

Venturing into the exciting realm of Xbox emulation gaming is akin to embarking on a journey through the annals of gaming history. Since its inception in 2001, the Xbox console has evolved into a stalwart presence in the gaming industry, offering a diverse range of immersive experiences. Thanks to the advancements in emulation technology, enthusiasts, gaming aficionados, and hobbyists now have the unique opportunity to relive the magic of Xbox games on their modern devices.

Emulation gaming, celebrated among retro console enthusiasts, extends its embrace to the Xbox. Through the amalgamation of specialized software and hardware, gamers can seamlessly play their favorite Xbox titles on PCs, laptops, or even handheld devices. This transformative experience liberates gaming enthusiasts from the constraints of the original console or the need for physical discs.

Handheld gaming console emulation has experienced a renaissance in recent years. The rise of powerful smartphones and portable gaming devices empowers enthusiasts to enjoy their beloved Xbox games on the go. Picture yourself navigating the expansive universe of Halo or delving into the fantastical realms of Fable during your daily commute—a testament to the endless possibilities offered by handheld Xbox emulation gaming.

Vintage computer emulation gaming, with its dedicated following, becomes a unique avenue within the Xbox emulation landscape. By emulating the Xbox on older computer systems, gamers can indulge in the nostalgia of playing Xbox titles on hardware from the past. This distinctive approach opens new doors for those who appreciate the historical tapestry and evolution of gaming.

Console-specific emulation, a vibrant niche in the emulation gaming community, is not confined to classic consoles alone. From revered icons like the NES and Sega Genesis to more recent additions like the Xbox 360, enthusiasts can traverse a vast library of games spanning various eras. This exploration allows gamers to unearth hidden gems, revisit childhood favorites, and even explore titles that were never released in their region.

Moreover, emulation gaming has found a meaningful place within educational settings. Employing Xbox emulation for educational purposes provides a novel and engaging platform for teachers to immerse students in interactive learning experiences. From historical simulations to problem-solving adventures, emulation gaming emerges as a dynamic tool for education, making learning a captivating journey.

In conclusion, Xbox emulation gaming unfolds a plethora of possibilities for gamers, enthusiasts, and hobbyists. Whether your aim is to rekindle the magic of classic Xbox titles, relish handheld gaming on the move, explore vintage computer gaming, or leverage emulation for educational pursuits, the avenues are limitless. Embrace the nostalgia, discover new experiences, and join the vibrant community of Xbox emulation gamers.

Exploring Other Console-Specific Emulation Options: A Panorama of Gaming Riches

In the expansive realm of emulation gaming, a myriad of options awaits to satiate the cravings of ardent gamers, enthusiasts, and hobbyists. While the surge of retro console emulation gaming has claimed its spotlight, other console-specific emulation options promise unique and thrilling experiences. Let's embark on a journey to explore these alternative choices and delve into the rich tapestry of possibilities they unfold.

Handheld gaming console emulation, a burgeoning niche, has steadily gained popularity. Emulators designed for iconic handheld consoles such as the Game Boy, Game Gear, and even the PlayStation Portable (PSP) allow gamers to relive portable gaming moments on computers or mobile devices. Whether it involves battling through Pokémon adventures or revisiting classics like Super Mario Land, handheld emulation offers a convenient and delightful way to experience these games without the need for physical hardware.

Vintage computer emulation gaming, a captivating avenue within the emulation landscape, beckons retro computer enthusiasts. By emulating classic systems like the Commodore 64, Amiga, or ZX Spectrum, gamers can immerse themselves in the golden age of computing. This journey involves recreating the software environment of these vintage machines, providing a glimpse into the rich library of games and software that defined an era.

Console-specific emulation, a cornerstone of emulation gaming, continues to captivate fans of classic gaming. Emulators tailored for iconic consoles like the NES, Sega Genesis, or PlayStation allow gamers to revisit legendary titles such as Super Mario Bros., The Legend of Zelda, Sonic the Hedgehog, and many more. With the ability to enhance graphics, improve performance, and introduce modern features like save states, console-specific emulation delivers a nostalgic yet enhanced gaming experience.

Beyond its role as a source of entertainment, emulation gaming emerges as a valuable tool for educational purposes. Emulators provide a unique opportunity to study the evolution of gaming technology and its profound impact on society. Educational institutions can leverage the power of emulation to teach students about the history of video games, programming, and computer architecture, fostering a deeper understanding of these subjects.

In conclusion, exploring other console-specific emulation options unfolds a world of possibilities for gamers, enthusiasts, and hobbyists. Handheld gaming console emulation, vintage computer emulation gaming, console-specific emulation, and even educational emulation gaming offer distinct experiences that cater to diverse interests. Whether you're reliving cherished memories, discovering hidden gems, or utilizing emulation as a conduit for learning, the vast landscape of emulation gaming welcomes all. So, grab your controllers and dive into the diverse realm of console-specific emulation, where the treasures of gaming history await your exploration!

| 6 |

Emulation Gaming for Educational Purposes

Benefits of Using Emulation Gaming for Education: A Gateway to Learning

In the dynamic world of gaming, emulation has emerged as a popular trend among gamers, enthusiasts, and hobbyists. Emulation gaming involves recreating or imitating a gaming console or computer system on different hardware. While it's widely appreciated for rekindling the nostalgia of retro and vintage gaming, its educational benefits are equally noteworthy.

One of the primary advantages of using

emulation gaming for education is the access it provides to an extensive library of games from different eras and platforms. Whether exploring retro console emulation gaming, handheld gaming console emulation, or vintage computer emulation gaming, emulation allows users to experience games that were once confined to specific hardware. This not only opens the door to a myriad of gaming experiences but also creates opportunities for learning about the evolution of gaming and its historical significance.

Emulation gaming serves as a unique tool for developing problem-solving and critical thinking skills. Many retro games are renowned for their challenging gameplay, requiring players to think strategically and overcome obstacles. Engaging with these games through emulation provides an avenue for players to hone cognitive abilities and learn to adapt to diverse gaming scenarios.

Moreover, emulation gaming has gained traction in schools and academic institutions. Console-specific emulation, such as NES or Sega Genesis, is recognized as a valuable educational tool. By integrating gaming into the curriculum, students can learn subjects like history, mathematics, and coding in an interactive manner. Emulation gaming provides a hands-on experience that fosters active learning and engagement.

Affordability and accessibility are additional benefits of emulation gaming. Unlike physical retro consoles or games, emulation gaming can be easily accessed through software on modern devices such as computers, smartphones, or dedicated handheld consoles. This accessibility simplifies the integration of emulation gaming into the learning journey without the need for expensive equipment or game cartridges.

In conclusion, the benefits of using emulation gaming for education are manifold. From accessing a diverse library of games to fostering problem-solving skills, emulation gaming offers a unique and engaging learning experience. Whether exploring retro console emulation gaming or utilizing console-specific emulation for educational purposes, emulation gaming has the potential to revolutionize the way we approach education. So, embrace the nostalgia, dive into the world of emulation gaming, and unlock the educational potential it holds.

Incorporating Emulation Gaming in the Classroom: A Paradigm Shift in Learning

Emulation gaming, a phenomenon that has captured the attention of gamers worldwide, is not merely a trip down memory lane; it's a transformative tool for education. In this subchapter, we explore the captivating concept of incorporating emulation gaming in the classroom, reshaping the landscape of teaching and learning.

Emulation gaming provides a unique opportunity to harmonize education and entertainment. By harnessing the power of retro console emulation gaming, handheld gaming console emulation, vintage computer emulation gaming, and console-specific emulation, educators can create an environment that captivates students of all ages.

The educational potential of emulation gaming is vast and varied. Teachers can immerse students in historical events through vintage computer emulation gaming, allowing them to experience the technological advancements of bygone eras. Students can explore different cultures and languages through console-specific emulation, playing games from diverse regions and gaining a nuanced understanding of global diversity.

Furthermore, emulation gaming contributes to the development of critical thinking and problem-solving skills. By challenging students to troubleshoot and configure emulators, they not only gain technical proficiency but also a deeper understanding of gaming systems. This hands-on approach nurtures curiosity and experimentation, fostering a growth mindset among students.

Collaboration and teamwork are integral components of emulation gaming in the classroom. Multiplayer games enable students to work together to achieve common goals, promoting communication, strategizing, and the development of social skills – crucial attributes for success in the contemporary world.

Emulation gaming serves as a gateway to STEAM (Science, Technology, Engineering, Arts, and Mathematics) education. Students can delve into programming and coding by creating their own emulators, modifying game code, or even designing their own games. This interdisciplinary approach not only enhances technical skills but also encourages creativity and innovation.

Incorporating emulation gaming in the classroom is a paradigm shift in education. By leveraging this technology, educators can create a dynamic and immersive learning environment that captivates and motivates students. Whether you're a gamer, gaming enthusiast, or gaming hobbyist, join us as we explore the world of emulation gaming and its potential to transform education.

Educational Resources and Tools for Emulation Gaming: Navigating the World of Knowledge

Emulation gaming has ushered in a revolution, offering gamers and enthusiasts a chance to relive the glory days of retro and vintage games.

Yet, beyond its nostalgic allure, emulation gaming stands as a valuable educational tool. In this sub-chapter, we delve into the diverse educational resources and tools available for emulation gaming, catering to a broad spectrum of interests within the gaming community.

For those stepping into the realm of emulation gaming, several comprehensive online platforms offer a wealth of educational resources. Websites like RetroArch and EmuParadise provide extensive libraries of ROMs, BIOS files, and emulators for various consoles and handheld devices. These platforms also offer tutorials, forums, and user guides to assist beginners in navigating the emulation process and addressing potential challenges.

Dedicated communities and forums focusing on specific niches within emulation gaming abound. Whether one's interest lies in retro console emulation, vintage computer emulation, or console-specific emulation, there are forums and communities where enthusiasts share knowledge, experiences, and resources. These platforms provide excellent opportunities to connect with like-minded individuals, seek advice, and discover hidden gems from gaming's past.

Emulation gaming's potential extends into educational settings, and specialized resources are available for educators. The Internet Archive's Software Library, for instance, houses a vast collection of vintage software, including educational games from the past. These resources enable educators to introduce students to the evolution of gaming and explore the cultural impact of video games.

In conclusion, emulation gaming offers a plethora of educational resources and tools for gamers, enthusiasts, and hobbyists. From comprehensive online platforms to niche communities and educational resources, there is something for everyone interested in exploring the world of emulation gaming. Whether you are a retro console enthusiast, a vintage computer aficionado, or a teacher looking to engage students in interactive learning experiences, emulation gaming provides an exciting and educational journey into the past.

Case Studies: Successful Implementation of Emulation Gaming in Education - Unveiling the Transformative Power

Emulation gaming, with its ability to blend entertainment and education seamlessly, has emerged as a transformative force in the realm of learning. In this subchapter, we delve into case studies that illuminate the successful implementation of emulation gaming in education. These real-world examples showcase how this innovative technology enhances learning experiences, captivates students, and deepens understanding across various subjects.

One compelling case study revolves around the integration of retro console emulation gaming in a history class. By immersing students in emulated games like "Oregon Trail" or "Civilization," historical events and scenarios were recreated. This hands-on approach made history more enjoyable and allowed students to actively participate, fostering critical thinking, problem-solving, and decision-making skills.

In a language arts class, handheld gaming

console emulation took center stage. Students engaged with classic games like "Pokémon" or "Final Fantasy" in their target language. This immersive experience not only made language learning more engaging but also facilitated practice in vocabulary, grammar, and reading comprehension. Significant improvements in language skills were observed among students.

Vintage computer emulation gaming found its place in education as well. By emulating old computer systems such as the Commodore 64 or Apple II, students delved into the evolution of technology, gaining insights into computer programming and coding. This case study highlighted how emulation gaming bridges the gap between the past and present, providing students with a unique perspective on the roots of modern technology.

Console-specific emulation, including NES or Sega Genesis, demonstrated its effectiveness in mathematics classes. Games requiring strategy and problem-solving were employed, allowing students to develop critical thinking skills while practicing mathematical concepts. The case study showcased how emulation gaming makes learning math enjoyable and accessible to a broader range of students.

A comprehensive case study explored the overall impact of emulation gaming across various subjects. By integrating emulation gaming into the curriculum, positive outcomes such as increased student engagement, improved academic performance, and a heightened passion for learning were observed. This holistic approach demonstrated the potential of emulation gaming to transform traditional learning methods.

In conclusion, these case studies exemplify the successful implementation of emulation gaming in education. From history to language arts, mathematics to computer programming, emulation gaming has become a powerful tool for educators. It not only breathes new life into traditional subjects but also makes learning exciting and accessible for gamers, gaming enthusiasts, and hobbyists. Emulation gaming, with its transformative power, continues to redefine the educational landscape, inspiring a new generation of learners.

Emulation Gaming Communities and Resources

Online Communities and Forums for Emulation Gaming: Connecting Enthusiasts Worldwide

In the vast landscape of emulation gaming, the internet has become a bustling hub where like-minded individuals converge to share experiences and explore the extensive universe of retro console, handheld, and vintage computer games. Online communities and forums dedicated to emulation gaming have blossomed into virtual meeting places for gamers, enthusiasts, and hobbyists, all seeking to relive the nostalgia of classic titles and uncover hidden gems from the past.

These digital platforms provide a space for gamers to interact, exchange knowledge, and find support for their emulation gaming endeavors. Whether you're a newcomer to emulation gaming or a seasoned player, these forums cater to a broad spectrum of interests within the emulation gaming community.

Enthusiasts of retro console emulation gaming can find dedicated forums focusing on specific consoles such as NES or Sega Genesis emulation. These platforms offer valuable resources, including tutorials on setting up emulators, troubleshooting common issues, and recommendations for must-play titles. Gamers can discuss their favorite games, share tips and tricks, and even engage in online multiplayer sessions through these communities.

Handheld gaming console emulation enthusiasts are not left behind, as specific online communities cater to their interests. These forums provide a wealth of information on emulating popular handheld consoles like the Game Boy or PSP. Members can explore the vast libraries of these portable consoles, discuss the best emulators and ROMs, and delve into homebrew games and fan-made modifications.

For those intrigued by vintage computer emulation gaming, dedicated communities celebrate the rich history of gaming on platforms like the Commodore 64 or the Amiga. These forums serve as a space for gamers to discuss their favorite retro computer games, share emulation setup guides, and relive the magic of classic gaming on these iconic machines.

The educational potential of emulation gaming has also carved out its space online. Communities focused on emulation gaming for educational purposes explore how it can be employed as a tool for learning history, programming, and game design. Members can delve into curated lists of educational games, share their experiences using emulation for educational purposes, and seek advice from fellow enthusiasts.

Whether you're a seasoned emulation gaming aficionado or just embarking on your journey into retro gaming, online communities and forums play a pivotal role in connecting gamers, providing resources, and fostering a sense of camaraderie. Join these communities, share your passion, and embark on a nostalgic adventure through the vast universe of emulation gaming.

Emulation Gaming Websites and Blogs: Portals to the Past and Present

In the expansive world of gaming, emulation gaming has emerged as a captivating phenomenon. This niche not only enthralls gamers, enthusiasts, and hobbyists by offering a trip down memory lane but also serves as a versatile tool for learning and exploration. To unravel the intricacies of emulation gaming, one must explore the plethora of knowledge and resources available on emulation gaming websites and blogs.

Emulation gaming websites function as comprehensive repositories of information, providing detailed guides on setting up emulators, configuring them to replicate specific consoles or computers, and troubleshooting any challenges that may arise. These platforms offer step-by-step instructions, often accompanied by visuals, ensuring that even the most novice users can navigate the process with ease. Additionally, these websites frequently feature forums and communities where gamers can connect, share experiences, and exchange tips and tricks.

Blogs dedicated to emulation gaming take a more personal and in-depth approach, offering articles and reviews that explore various facets of emulation gaming. They may delve into topics such as the best emulators for different consoles, recommended games to play, hidden gems to discover, and even feature interviews with developers and enthusiasts. These blogs serve as a treasure trove of nostalgia, providing a platform for passionate writers to share their love for retro gaming and educate readers about the history and significance of different gaming platforms.

Emulation gaming websites and blogs also play

a crucial role in promoting the educational benefits of emulation gaming. They highlight how teachers and educators can leverage these tools to create interactive and engaging lessons, allowing students to explore the evolution of technology and gaming. From grasping the fundamental principles of programming to experiencing the cultural impact of iconic games, emulation gaming offers a unique educational experience that transcends traditional teaching methods.

In conclusion, emulation gaming websites and blogs have become indispensable resources for gamers, enthusiasts, and hobbyists. They provide a wealth of information, support, and a sense of community in the vast world of emulation gaming. Whether you are a retro console aficionado, a handheld gaming enthusiast, a vintage computer gaming aficionado, or even a teacher looking to incorporate interactive learning experiences, these platforms offer invaluable insights and guidance. Explore the world of emulation gaming through these websites and blogs, and embark on a journey of nostalgia, discovery, and education.

Recommended Emulation Gaming Software and Tools: Elevating Your Gaming Experience

In the realm of emulation gaming, having the right software and tools is paramount to recreating the nostalgia and excitement of playing retro games. Whether you're a seasoned gamer, a gaming enthusiast, or a gaming hobbyist, this subchapter, titled "Recommended Emulation Gaming Software and Tools," aims to provide you with a comprehensive list of tools and software that will enhance your emulation gaming experience.

1. RetroArch: Widely regarded as one of the most versatile and comprehensive emulation software, RetroArch supports a broad range of consoles and platforms. It boasts a user-friendly interface, customizable controls, and an extensive library of games to choose from.

2. Dolphin: Tailored for fans of Nintendo GameCube and Wii games, Dolphin stands out as a premier emulator. It offers high-definition graphics, support for various controllers, and additional features like save states and cheat codes.

3. VisualBoy Advance: The go-to emulator for handheld gaming console enthusiasts, VisualBoy Advance specializes in Game Boy, Game Boy Color, and Game Boy Advance games. It delivers excellent compatibility, fast gameplay, and customizable controls.

4. DOSBox: For those interested in vintage computer emulation gaming, DOSBox is an essential tool. It enables the running of old DOS-based games on modern systems, preserving the original experience, and provides options for tweaking graphics and sound settings.

5. Higan: This top-notch emulator focuses on console-specific emulation, including NES, Super NES, Game Boy, and more. Higan is known for its accurate emulation, high compatibility, and advanced features like ROM hacking and netplay.

6. MAME (Multiple Arcade Machine Emulator):

Ideal for recreating the arcade experience at home, MAME supports a vast collection of arcade games. It enables enthusiasts to relive classics without the need for bulky arcade cabinets.

7. ScummVM: Dedicated to point-and-click adventure games, ScummVM is a must-have emulator. It supports numerous classic titles from developers like LucasArts and Sierra, providing a seamless experience on modern systems.

8. MinecraftEdu: Illustrating the educational potential of emulation gaming, MinecraftEdu offers an educational version of Minecraft. It allows students to learn and explore various subjects in a fun and interactive way.

These recommended emulation gaming software and tools cater to a wide range of niches, including retro console emulation gaming, handheld gaming console emulation, vintage computer emulation gaming, console-specific emulation, and even emulation gaming for educational purposes. By utilizing these tools, you can dive into the world of emulation gaming and relive the magic of retro games while enjoying modern conveniences and enhancements.

Legal and Ethical Considerations in Emulation Gaming: Navigating the Gray Areas

As the world of gaming continues its dynamic evolution, one segment that has captured significant attention is emulation gaming. Enabling players to experience classic retro games on modern devices, emulation gaming evokes nostalgia and preserves gaming history. However, this captivating realm of gaming is not without its own set of legal and ethical considerations, demanding awareness from gamers and enthusiasts alike.

From a legal standpoint, the emulation gaming community often treads a fine line concerning copyright infringement. Emulators, which replicate the functionality of gaming consoles, and ROMs, copies of game cartridges, are typically protected by copyright laws. While the distribution and downloading of copyrighted ROMs is illegal, the legality of owning and utilizing emulators varies from country to country. It is crucial for gamers to comprehend the laws in their jurisdiction and ensure they engage in legal activities.

Ethically, gamers should also consider the impact of emulation gaming on the industry. While playing retro games through emulation can be a fun and educational experience, it is essential to support game developers and publishers by purchasing legitimate copies of games whenever possible. Emulation gaming should not be viewed as a replacement for buying games but rather as a means to preserve gaming history and experience titles that may be otherwise inaccessible.

Another ethical consideration revolves around the preservation of gaming culture. Emulation gaming allows enthusiasts to explore vintage computer games, console-specific titles, and handheld gaming experiences that might not be available on modern platforms. By engaging in emulation gaming, players contribute to the preservation of gaming history, ensuring that future generations can appreciate the roots of the industry.

Additionally, emulation gaming for educational purposes has gained traction in recent years. Teachers and educators have adopted this technology to introduce students to the history of gaming, programming, and computer science. Emulators provide a valuable tool for understanding the evolution of technology and the cultural impact of gaming.

In conclusion, while emulation gaming offers a unique and exciting way to revisit classic games, it is essential to be mindful of the legal and ethical considerations surrounding this niche. By understanding and respecting copyright laws, supporting game developers, and preserving gaming culture, gamers and enthusiasts can fully enjoy the world of emulation gaming while still upholding the integrity of the gaming industry.

| 8 |

Future Trends and Developments in Emulation Gaming

Advances in Emulation Technology: Nostalgia Enhanced by Innovation

In the ever-evolving realm of gaming, technology serves as a catalyst for change, and one area that has seen remarkable progress is emulation technology. This subchapter explores the cutting-edge advances in emulation technology, transforming the way gamers experience retro console games, vintage computer games, and handheld gaming console titles.

Retro console emulation gaming has become a phenomenon, allowing gamers to revisit cherished memories by playing classic games from consoles like the NES and Sega Genesis. Thanks to advancements in emulation technology, these experiences are now more authentic than ever. Emulation software has evolved to accurately replicate original hardware, delivering an immersive retro gaming encounter.

Handheld gaming console emulation has undergone significant improvements. Emulators now support popular handheld consoles such as Game Boy, Game Boy Advance, and even the iconic PSP. Versatile and accessible, these emulators enable gamers to enjoy their favorite handheld games on PCs, smartphones, or dedicated handheld devices designed for emulation gaming.

Vintage computer emulation gaming has not lagged behind. Advanced emulation software allows gamers to explore the vast library of classic computer games from platforms like the Commodore 64, Amiga, and MS-DOS. These emulators faithfully recreate the computing environments of the past, offering an authentic glimpse into the golden age of computer gaming.

Beyond entertainment, emulation gaming has found educational applications. Emulation technology empowers educators to leverage classic games as engaging learning tools. Students can delve into historical events through historically accurate games or grasp programming concepts by studying the code of classic games. Emulation technology has added a new dimension to education, making it more interactive for students.

As the demand for emulation gaming continues to rise, technology keeps pace. Emulation software developers consistently push boundaries, seeking innovative ways to enhance the gaming experience. With each passing year, we can anticipate more accurate and feature-rich emulators, catering to the diverse needs and desires of the gaming community.

In conclusion, the advances in emulation technology have reshaped the gaming landscape, providing gamers, enthusiasts, and hobbyists with an opportunity to relive the glory days of gaming. Retro console emulation, handheld gaming console emulation, vintage computer emulation, and console-specific emulation have all benefited from these advancements. Furthermore, emulation gaming has found a place in education, enriching the learning experience for students. Looking ahead, we can expect even more exciting developments in emulation technology, promising a more immersive and authentic gaming experience for all.

Potential Impact of Virtual Reality on Emulation Gaming: Bridging the Past and Future

Virtual reality (VR) stands as a revolutionary technology across various industries, and gaming is no exception. The fusion of VR and emulation gaming holds the potential to provide an entirely new level of immersive experiences for gamers, enthusiasts, and hobbyists. In this subchapter, we explore the potential impact of virtual reality on emulation gaming and how it can elevate the already captivating world of retro gaming.

Emulation gaming, dedicated to recreating the gaming experiences of bygone eras, has garnered a dedicated following. With the introduction of virtual reality, enthusiasts can immerse themselves in their favorite classic characters and explore familiar pixelated landscapes in an unprecedented way. Imagine donning a VR headset and finding yourself transported into the vibrant streets of Mushroom Kingdom or the treacherous dungeons of Hyrule, all while reliving the golden age of gaming.

One of the key advantages of VR in emulation gaming is its ability to provide a more authentic experience. By placing players in a virtual world, VR eliminates the barrier between the gamer and the game, creating a truly immersive experience. Whether it's the feel of a retro controller or the visual aesthetics of a vintage console, VR can recreate these elements, making gamers feel as if they are playing on the original hardware.

Furthermore, VR has the potential to enhance the educational aspect of emulation gaming. By combining the nostalgic appeal of retro games with the immersive power of virtual reality, educators can create interactive learning experiences. Students can explore historical events through the lens of retro games, gaining a deeper understanding of the past while enjoying the educational process.

While the potential of VR in emulation gaming is exciting, challenges remain. Emulation gaming often involves recreating the hardware and software of old gaming systems, and ensuring compatibility with virtual reality technology can be complex. Additionally, considerations about the preservation and legality of emulation gaming remain crucial.

In conclusion, the integration of virtual reality into emulation gaming has the potential to redefine the gaming landscape for gamers, enthusiasts, and hobbyists. By providing an immersive experience and enhancing the educational potential, VR can take emulation gaming to new heights. As technology continues to advance, it is an exciting time for gamers to explore the endless possibilities awaiting them in the fusion of virtual reality and emulation gaming.

Emulation Gaming in the Age of Cloud Gaming: Breaking the Chains of Physical Hardware

As technology advances at an exponential rate, the gaming landscape has undergone a significant transformation. The age of cloud gaming has ushered in a new era for emulation gaming, making it easier than ever to access a vast library of retro games from various consoles and handheld devices. In this subchapter, we explore how cloud gaming has influenced emulation gaming, breaking the chains of physical hardware and offering gamers unparalleled accessibility.

Retro console emulation gaming has become a popular niche within the gaming community. With the ability to replicate the experience of playing on a classic console, complete with original controllers and visual filters, gamers can relive their childhood memories in stunning detail. The nostalgia factor alone attracts gaming enthusiasts and hobbyists who long for the simpler times of pixelated graphics and 8-bit soundtracks.

Cloud gaming platforms have made it possible to access a diverse range of retro games without the need for physical hardware. Gamers can enjoy classics from the NES, Sega Genesis, and even vintage computer games with just a few clicks. This newfound accessibility has democratized retro gaming, allowing players to experience the magic of classic titles without the constraints of physical consoles and cartridges.

Handheld gaming console emulation takes the experience a step further, allowing gamers to enjoy their favorite Game Boy, PSP, or even Nintendo DS games on their smartphones or tablets. The convenience of carrying a vast library of games in your pocket has revolutionized how gamers approach handheld gaming, all made possible through the convenience of cloud gaming.

Emulation gaming, traditionally associated with

desktops and specialized hardware, has now become more versatile thanks to cloud gaming. The barriers to entry have been lowered, and gamers can engage in emulation experiences across a variety of devices, from powerful gaming PCs to lightweight laptops and even smartphones.

But emulation gaming isn't just about entertainment; it can also be a powerful tool for education. Many educators have recognized the potential of using emulation gaming to teach history, cultural studies, and even coding. By exploring the games of the past, students can gain a deeper understanding of the evolution of technology and its impact on society.

In conclusion, the integration of emulation gaming into the age of cloud gaming has unlocked new possibilities for gamers, enthusiasts, and hobbyists. Whether you're seeking a nostalgic trip down memory lane or an educator looking for innovative ways to engage students, the world of emulation gaming in the age of cloud gaming has something to offer. So, grab your virtual controller and embark on a journey through the pixelated wonders of the past. The future of gaming awaits!

Predictions for the Future of Emulation Gaming: A Glimpse into Gaming Evolution

In the ever-evolving world of gaming, emulation gaming has emerged as a captivating phenomenon. As technology advances and the demand for retro gaming experiences continues to grow, the future of emulation gaming holds tremendous potential. In this subchapter, we delve into predictions for the future of emulation gaming, anticipating exciting developments that will shape the gaming landscape.

One prediction is the continued expansion of retro console emulation. The insatiable demand for classic gaming experiences indicates that the emulation community will respond with even more accurate emulators. This means gamers will have access to a broader array of retro consoles, from the iconic NES and Sega Genesis to lesser-known systems, all in one convenient place.

Handheld gaming console emulation is expected to experience significant growth. With portable devices becoming increasingly powerful, emulating handheld gaming consoles such as the Game Boy, Game Gear, and PlayStation Portable on a variety of devices will become more prevalent. This opens up a whole new world of gaming experiences for players on the go, making it easier than ever to enjoy their favorite handheld games wherever they are.

Vintage computer emulation is poised to thrive as well. As older computer systems become more challenging to find and maintain, emulation provides a viable alternative for enthusiasts to explore the rich history of computing. From the early days of DOS to iconic machines like the Commodore 64 and Amiga, vintage computer emulation allows gamers to experience the software and games that defined an era.

Console-specific emulation, such as NES or Sega Genesis emulation, is expected to flourish further. Developers will create specialized emulators for specific systems, ensuring even greater accuracy and compatibility. This level of speciali-zation will provide players with the most authen-tic gaming experiences possible, catering to the unique needs and desires of gamers.

Emulation gaming for educational purposes will continue to gain traction. The ability to emu-late historical systems and games offers educators and students a unique opportunity to explore the evolution of technology and gaming. Emulation can serve as a valuable tool for teaching program-ming, game design, and even history, allowing students to engage with the past in a hands-on and interactive way.

In conclusion, the future of emulation gaming is bright and promising. With advancements in technology and the growing demand for retro gaming experiences, gamers, enthusiasts, and hob-byists can look forward to a wide range of excit-ing developments. From expanded retro console emulation to specialized console-specific emula-tors, the possibilities are endless. So, get ready to embark on a journey through gaming history and experience the best of both worlds – the nostalgia of classic games and the convenience of modern devices.

| 9 |

Final Thoughts

Recap of Key Points

In the exploration of emulation gaming, we've covered various aspects catering to gamers, enthusiasts, and hobbyists. "Pixel Pioneers: Exploring the World of Emulation Gaming" has taken us through retro console emulation gaming, handheld gaming console emulation, vintage computer emulation gaming, console-specific emulation, and emulation gaming for educational purposes. Let's recap the key points:

1. Retro Console Emulation Gaming:

- Emulation allows gamers to experience classics from consoles like NES and Sega Genesis on modern devices.

- Emulators and ROMs provide a means to relive nostalgic gaming moments and preserve gaming history.

2. Handheld Gaming Console Emulation:

- Opportunities to play Game Boy, PSP, and other handheld classics on everyday devices.

- Emulators and BIOS files are crucial for a smooth gaming experience, with legal and ethical considerations surrounding ROM acquisition.

3. Vintage Computer Emulation Gaming:

- Emulation enables the experience of software and games from platforms like DOS, Amiga, and more on modern machines.

- Significance lies in preserving vintage systems and their software for future generations.

4. Console-Specific Emulation:

- Focus on popular platforms like NES and Sega Genesis with various emulators offering unique features and compatibility.

- Choosing the right emulator is crucial for an authentic and enjoyable gaming experience.

5. Emulation Gaming for Educational Purposes:

- Emulation serves as an interactive tool for

exploring historical artifacts, virtual museums, and educational settings.

- Educators use emulation to teach programming, problem-solving, and critical thinking skills.

Final Thoughts on Emulation Gaming

Emulation gaming, beyond providing a haven for nostalgia, stands as a powerful tool for education and preservation. It allows gamers to reconnect with childhood memories, offers alternatives for experiencing classic games, and ensures these games are not lost to time. Emulation also plays a significant role in education, teaching valuable skills and providing a gateway to understanding technology and its impact on society.

Resources for Further Exploration

For those eager to delve deeper into emulation gaming, there are abundant resources to enhance knowledge and experience:

1. Online Communities and Forums: Engage in platforms like Reddit and Discord to connect with enthusiasts, share experiences, and discover new games and emulators.

2. Emulator Websites: Explore sites like Retro-Arch, EmuParadise, and CoolROM for a wide range of emulators and tools.

3. Retro Gaming Expos and Conventions: Attend events featuring retro gaming tournaments, discussions, and opportunities to meet industry experts.

4. YouTube Channels and Twitch Streams: Discover content creators showcasing gameplay, reviewing emulators, and offering insights into retro gaming.

5. Documentation and Online Archives: Explore resources on websites like The Emulation Wiki and the Internet Archive for technical information and historical documentation.

6. Educational Resources: Utilize educational platforms like The Learning Network for articles and lesson plans incorporating retro gaming.

7. Developer Communities: Join GitHub and SourceForge for open-source emulation projects and collaboration opportunities.

Always prioritize legal and ethical considerations, respecting copyright laws and ensuring device safety. With these resources, enthusiasts can embark on a journey through emulation gaming, rediscovering classics, and gaining insights into gaming history and technology. Happy gaming!

9 7 9 8 8 6 9 0 7 9 6 1 9